UDAAN

EK PANCHHI KI

SHRISHTI AGARWAL

Made with ♥ on the Notion Press Platform
www.notionpress.com

This Book is dedicated to my Brother In law- Vivek Sharma, who inspired me to write. You left us way too soon but I am sure you will be happy that I wrote this one. We miss you!

Contents

Foreword

My Husband asked me, why do you think people will want to read your book! I said two things- One, it's the story of a women who has done wonders in her life but fails to acknowledge it. Her story needs to be told to the world, for her life is full of inspiration and motivation.

And second, this book is written by her daughter in law, defying the odds that this relationship cannot go along. So go through her life journey with me. I hope by the end of the book, you have smile on your face, love in your heart and strength in your mind.

Foreword

Preface

No writer should say this, but it's the truth. Writing this Book was never in the plan.

Yeah ! Growing up with two amazing women i.e. my mom and my elder sister, I never had to look far for inspiration. It was right there for me. But I never knew that after marriage as well, I would find my pillar of strength, My Mother In law, a.k.a Panchhi and would be writing about her.

A very common notion that we generally hear is that a Mother In law and a Daughter in law can never get along, and this book breaks that stigma. We share a very different relation. We are more like friends who understand each other, are there for each other and motivate each other. In other words, I am Blessed.

In the past 4 years that I have known her, I am always amazed at the way she carries herself. Her stories are always fun to hear and gradually the idea of this book came into picture. Like I said, it was never in the plan. My Husband filled in with a lot more details about her, helping me get even more inspired and I became all the sure about this book.

Everytime she tells me about some event of her life, some incident, I cannot tell how amazing it feels. I thought about it, how each and every phase in her life has so much to learn from and her I am , writing this book. You see, the world always looks up for inspiration and I really hope this book can provide that.

This book has chapters and each chapter is one phase of her life. Allow me to take you through her life story.

CHAPTER ONE

CHILDHOOD

Born to a Punjabi Family in Dehradun, Panchhi is the second child to them. An elder sister, and two younger siblings, she was always very different from others. Oh, her real name is Harbans kaur. She is called Panchhi, probably owing to her free spirit.

Her father (Papa ji) was a very strong, powerful man who had his say back then in the society. I now know where she gets her strength from. Her mom (Jhai Ji) was a very simple lady who was high on principles and values. They build their empire from scratch as her father and mother were refugees from Pakistan, who had riches over there, but during partition, they came to India and started their life again.

He owned a Food cart in Dehradun. And owing to that, yes, the entire family has food in their blood. No wonder both my Mother in law and my husband cook so well.

Anyways, giving the background of her family, let me take you through her childhood. It was a very different childhood that she had.

Her Dad always knew that they had to teach and educate their kids no matter what, but from a very young age, Panchhi understood and overtook a lot of responsibilities at home.

So she along with her elder sister would wake up around 4 AM every morning, help her dad in the food business by doing all the preparations before hand. He used to run a food cart of Chole Bhature, which is a famous punjabi dish. So this preparation would include preparing chole, making the dough and then preparing bhature , packing it all and then cleaning the entire kitchen and house. Mind you, this preparation would include close to 1500-2000 Bhature and approximately 10 kgs of Chole!!! All this had to be done every single day. They knew that their dad needs their help and they need to support their family.

Post this, she would have her brealfast and rush to school. Going to school was important and she knew it. And unlike in today's time, she would walk to school which was easily some 2-3 kms from her home.

This was a daily routine. Be it a weekday or a weekend, this was a daily work for her. At days, when the demand was higher, after school as well she would need to prepare the food. She never complained or cribbed about it, infact did this all work with dedication. Makes you thing right, how priveleged we were and are.

But apart from all this work, she knew how to have fun! She had a knack for stiching, decoration and a lot of creative stuff and so, she would get involved in that. She made bedhseets for home, stiched curtains, made home decor stuff and a lot more.

She tells me, every now and then, she would change the setting of the house, arrange stuff in a different manner and her dad would be like, go change the house exterior also... kidding to her!

That creativity is still there. She has knacks for small and big things and I am always amazed by that.

She was and is a neat freak and that would distinguish her from everyone else in her family. She would always want her home to look clean, neat and tidy and so, even after all that work (cooking, school and everything else) , she would have the energy to clean the home again at night before sleeping. Phew!!! She tells me, I am not like any of my family members, parents included when it comes to cleanliness.

If anyone of her favorite TV shows/movie would be broadcasted, she would just finish all the work beforehand just in time for the show and then sit back and watch the show. She tells me that during new year eve, unlike now, they all i.e. her family, neighbors and close friends would gather around at their home, they would have popcorn, peanuts, Chikki etc, all cozied up and would watch some program on TV that would air for New year eve. It kind of became like a tradition for them.

And not just that, she always knew the importance of money, right from the start and has taught me about the same now. She tells me, from the pocket money she would get to eat in school, she would save some of it and when it became a substantial amount, she and her sister would go buy sofa, curtains for home, as she was very fond of the same and I tell her, you would have made a very good Interior designer.

She tells me, how she was fond of new clothes and how she would save them for some special occasion. And also how her elder sister would wear those and step out. She says, very often when she would return from school, she would find the house locked. Her mom and her sister would go for a movie and she would just wait for them outside the house, all upset and then she would get super angry when she would see that her sister wore her new suit. When I asked her, why didn't you wear her clothes, she said, her clothes would not fit me, but my clothes would fit her. We would laught out loud at it. Typical siblings love and rivalry you see!

Oh and the picnics- No, not like you and I had when we were kids. Those picnics were next level. She tells how they would hire a mini bus, gather all their relatives and neighbours and go to different places nearby. But, with a twist. They would carry stove, gas cylinders and raw materials and once they reached the destination, her papa Ji would cook for everyone. They all would relish the food, relax and then would be back to home. At times, they would make fire on the spot , get veggies and chicken and would barbeque and enjoy. Well, that's how it is supposed to be right. We have seem to forgotten the right way of doing certain things.

Listening to her childhood stories always makes me think, no matter how hard it was for her, whenever she narrates the story, there is always a smile on her face. She would always tell each detail happily with no regrets whatsover. I mean that attitude is unremarkable.

After her school, she completed her Graduation and Post Graduation. She is a Economics Graduate. She even did B.Ed . She did wanted to work post her studies, but her dad would say, I will teach you all you want, but the decision of you working would be on your, to be, In laws. She made peace with it, afterall her dad supported her in every other thing. You would see an amazing example of that in the next few paragraphs.

She continued helping her dad on his business front and her mom on household chores. She even took care of her younger siblings and that can be seen in the bond they share now also. Not just that, her neice and nephews are super fond of her. They say, Panchhi is more like a mother to us. In their childhood, Panchhi took care of them, fed them and played with them. I can still see that bond between them.

Back then, or even now, getting a girl married after she completes her studies was like the obvious thing to do. So the same was happening to her. Let me tell you a very interesting story here. There was an alliance for her from some place around Dehradun and a known relative was supposed to take her there since her Papa Ji and Jhai Ji were out of town. Unwillingly she went there and was so annoyed after meeting the family that she decided to run from there. Like for real. Luckily, her uncle got to know and said, its okay, I will drop you back home, don't go alone!!!

She came back home and said no for that alliance and her parents never questioned that. To be honest, I would never have such guts. She is courageous, I give you that!

In all this process of meeting guys for her marriage, something changed . Seeing her friends and relatives after marriage, and how their life changed, and not for good, she somehow never wanted to get married. She would be like I am better off without it. She even told her parents about her decision to never get married and to her unbelief, they supported her 100 percenatge, no questions asked. Let me remind you, this is from a time, when getting daughters married off was the only thing parents had on their mind.

She said, I will teach, earn and live my life my way. They said, yes you do that and we will have a separte floor build for you in this home and you can stay there and live your life.

I was blown off, when I heard this story. Having this mindset at that young age and having such cool parents who would support you, is not something you get to hear so often, even in today's time!

But, Life had different plans for her. Afterall, had she not gotten married, I and this book would not have been there in her life.

My father in law used to stay few houses away from her house. He used to come home to teach her younger brother and like any bollywood movie, thats how their love story started and I guess knowing him all those years, she said yes to him and they got married. A Love Marriage!

That was Panchhi's childhood for you. Full of ups and downs but she cherishes each and every moment of it. She often says, Childhood was the best time of my life. No tensions, no stress and doing whatever you feel like.

When I look back to her childhood, I believe there is a lot to learn from that. How to take a stand, how to find time to do your thing that you love, how to be passionate, compassionate and strong at the same time, how to find joys in the smallest of thing and a lot more. Its all about the attitude and perspective one has in life. When she narrates any incident from her childhood, there is always a smile and happiness in her face.

I admire her attitude towards life and I know in the coming chapters we would see more of it.

CHAPTER TWO

LIFE AFTER MARRIAGE

As they say, the things you run away from the most is the thing you always end up doing. And so was the case with Panchhi. From being sure of never getting married , Panchhi then married the love of her life. When Panchhi got married, her In laws had a tradion where the Daughter-In-Law gets a new name. Yeah and so Harbans kaur became Rashmi Sharma but Panchhi and her spirit remained the same. Till date, her siblings and relatives call her Panchhi.

My Father in Law used to work with a Government Bank and had a transferrable job. Panchhi's Mother in Law also stayed with them. While Panchhi always wanted to work after marriage, but due to household responsibilities and duties, she could never actually do that.

Right from the start, she had to take care of her Mother in law who was physically not in a very good shape and take care of everything else in her home. Being in a transferrable job, they moved cities and houses quite often. Every 3 years or so, they would change cities and Panchhi would find herself in a new place, with a different culture and amongst different people. While many may find it annoying and difficult, she always welcomed the change. She would look forward to meeting new people, learning from them and knowing about their life.

And in that journey, she has lived in various Indian cities starting with Aligarh and then moved around to Meerut, Udaipur, Jodhpur, Ahemdabad, Lucknow, Dehardun, Patna..

While Father in law was away at work, she would stay back home and handle the home, kids and everything else. With every changing city, came new challenges. Extreme weather conditions, house space limitation, house help availability, making friends again etc etc, but she being she, accepted it all very gracefully and found solutions to all her problems.

She tells me how from every other city she has stayed in, she has learned something or the other. She learnt about different cuisines, different languages, festivals, culture and what not. And till date, she is in touch with few of her friends who she met in this journey.

I would like to stress on this part. For our mothers, specially who were homemakers, having friends around was so important. And I am glad, till date, even after so many transfers, she has few of them still in touch with her. Feels good you know.

Her favourite place amongst all is Udaipur. It's a beautiful city, undoubtedly. She tells me how Uncle would take her to lakes, that she loved. Her house was also well airy, open and had a veranda where her mother in law would sit. Everything was perfect, the home, the city and the feel.

When I ask her which place she did not like- she says: every place had its pros and cons. But one place she had a complicated relationship was Ahemdabad. Well, initially it was tough for her. I will tell you why! Right from her childhood, to places after marriage, utill they moved to Ahemdabad, Panchhi had always stayed in an Independent house/Bungalow which basically had open lawn/terrace, a space to come out of the house and move around without actually needing to stepping out of the house. Now, in Ahemdabad, they were given office aparments which was close to the bank. This was the very first time that she had to stay in an apartment, which was really claustrophobic for her. She would yearn to go out as freely as she could do with other places.

Her Anxiety kicked in and it became really difficult for her. She tells me how she literally cried when she found that she needs to stay in there. She would take Manu out in the night when she couldn't sleep and would spend hours roaming outside, in the society premises. Then would come back and sleep off. So, yes it was really difficult but despite that , she never cribbed. She learnt how to manage in the apartment, made friends to help ease the process, learnt a lot of gujrati cuisines and the most difficult place became her next favourite.

Despite the anxiety, this was the place wherein the inclusion helped her big time. People would come together and celebarte all the festivals together, organize meet ups for everyone. She really loved that and was able to bond with everyone. So much, that when they were leaving Ahemdabad, she bought gifts for all her friends and was crying inconsolably. She says- that time won't come back and nor will those people, but these are memories that she will cherish forver.

Let me take you back on this Anxiety thing. This wasn't just because of the move to an apartment. It started during her 1st pregnancy, when she was expecting Manu (her elder son, my husband). Almost at the end of the pregnancy, there was someone very close to her who passed away, and the family, being protective, decided not to tell her, so that she could deliver the baby without any stress. But somehow, soon after the delivery, she got to know and that came as a Shock to her- one about the news and second that she wasn't told. Since this, this anxiety had been there and she kept finding ways to deal with it.

She had psychiatric consultations, but the treatment was never on track and somehow root cause wasn't tackled. The problem kept lingering but more about this in the later section of the book.

Meanwhile, uncle started building their own home in Dehradun. Pannchi always wanted to live there and they designed the home keeping everyone in mind. Uncle also got a transfer to Dehradun and so she was super excited to be living in her home. Just when their stuff had arrived, uncle got to know that he has been transferred to Lucknow.

Pannchi knew that they will have to move to Lucknow and her wish of staying in her own home will be postponed. And there it was, one more unfullfilled dream but no regrets Pannchi had. They did the house warming and then moved to the new city.

Life kept on happening. She raised her 2 sons, learned to travel alone, at times with just the kids, basically adapted to the life she had.

Her Elder son (Manu Sharma) went off to study in college, while her younger one (Vivek Sharma) completed his studies.

She tells me about how in Ahemdabad, they all would savour Dosa and Icecreams, how she learnt about Dabeli. How, in Lucknow, she went to the street vendor, stood there and learnt how to make Chowmein because Vicky was so fond of it and how in Patna, she made sattu paratha, litti etc. etc. So, yes, apart from everything else, her love for cooking food, learning about new dishes remained constant. And yes, you will hear more about her love for cooking later in the book.

In one of her stories, that I could not stop laughing about. She says, how in Lucknow they had just moved in. And once after getting Vicky back from school she was coming in a rickshow. Now, since she was fairly new there, she got confused with the way to home and wandered around the colony for almost 3 hrs. before she could spot her house.

She still tells thats story and we all laugh.

Vivek (vicky) was born with a hole in his heart and so during his studies, he underwent a procedure but later, finally at the age of 18, underwent a surgery. Panchhi stayed with him in Gurgaon for his studies and treatment, while father in law was posted in Alwar, so either he would come down to meet them or she would travel to Alwar. Those 2 years of juggling between places was difficult but Panchhi knew her responsibilities well enough.

Staying in Gurgaon, her nieces encouraged her to take a job at one of the child daycare centers. They prepped her for the interview and she nailed it. They were so impressed with her and she was selected. Her niece would drop her to the daycare while going to office and would pick her up while coming back. Panchhi was amazing with the kids. The owner also praised her. She was enjoying that. But later, due to some clashes there, she decided to leave that job. She didn't even went to take the salary for those few months she worked there.

Later when Vicky also went off to college, father in law got transferred to Patna. Panchhi tells me about her struggles there, how their stuff got delayed, how the house would get flooded in rains but she also tells me how she learned about Sattu (gram flour powder), how their home was walking distance from the airport (her sister once walked and reached home.. so awesome right) and how she found peace with the place. She also made an amazing friend here, who she is still in touch with.

Everything seemed normal, on track, with Manu starting his Job in Kolkata to vicky pursuing his studies, things were good. Panchhi also had a good routine there in Patna, with her walks, shopping, chit-chatting. But apparently, Life had other plans.

One of the days, while doing his daily, routine work, my father in law started noticing some issues such as uncontrolled motor movements, issue with balance etc. Upon consulting a doctor and getting tests done, he was diagnosed with Huntington Disease, which is a rare genetic disease. It shows up in the later years of one's life and is un-treatable. There are things which can be done to subside the effects, but yes, there is no treatment for it till date.

Upon learning about Hunginton and how it would impact his daily work, my father in law decided to take a Voluntary retirement from his job and Manu bought them back to Kolkata with him so that he could work and take care of his Dad alongside.

Again as fate had it, Panchhi found herself in a new city,new culture, new traditions but how beautifully she adjusted there and made it her next new home. The one thing she loved about Kolkata was how they had parks/ gardens in every short distance and how much she loved walking there.

Hungtington is a rare disease, especially in India and so the required specialized help is not everywhere. So now to learn more about treatment options, guidance and for further helping his dad, Manu decided to move to Bangalore as NIMHANS is one place where they have research going on over Hungtington and they would get better help there. For this, he looked for a job in Bangalore and then the family moved to Bangalore.

Panchhi now was in a city that was very different. This was her first time in the southern part of the country. Language barrier, different food habits, different crowd but she being she, adjsuted so well in the city. She found places nearby to get grocery, veggies, pooja stuff and what not.

Good part- Manu's college best friend was settled in Bangalore, so there was a known face in this new city.

Bad part- Panchhi's start in Bangalore wasn't great. In the first week of their moving, she had bad allergic reaction and had developed rashes. The next week itself, while going to a temple, she fell down and broke both of her wrists, which took almost 3-4 weeks to heal properly. And to top it off, her anxiety started kicking in again. Once she had to be taken to ER for her anxiety so yeah, Bangalore was super difficult for her in the start. But like I said, she knew her responsibilities well and so made peace with Bangalore.

A different phase of her life began, where she would stay with my father in law, go out to get groceries and also make lunch tiffin for Manu. Our Indian Mom's are amazing no. No matter how old you get, if she is at home, you gotta take the tiffin to work.

Gradually, Uncle's treatment started. The family got to know more about Huntington. Till this time, Vicky had also completed his studies and had started working in Chennai so even he would visit more often.

Panchhi got involved in Uncle's care, along with taking care of the kids. They even hired a full time help for an extra helping hand. Now, again when things looked manageable, another incident happened. Uncle was diagnosed with Oral Cancer.

Being in Bangalore, Manu was able to find the right help and uncle underwent chemotherapy, surgery and radiation for his treatment. Panchhi would accompany him for his chemo sessions, she stood like a rock with him, when he needed that support. She would travel hours daily for the chemo sessions.

Not just that, Manu had arranged for counselling, nutritionist during uncle's treatment and Panchhi would get involved everywhere. She is very open to all the new age techniques/ways to combat. She knows with time, one needs to evolve and she did the same. She would talk to the counsellors, nutritionist and make changes as needed. I was amazed when I got to know of this.

Now, post the surgery and the treatment , uncle could not eat directly and so Panchhi would find ways to feed him healthy, nutritious and tasty food. He was a on strict diet and panchhi would ensure that he gets all the required nutrition and would innovate and find ways to feed him.

With all the love and care, his treatment went well and the reports came out good and he was cancer free. The family was relieved. A lot of relatives also visited them, which gave Panchhi and everyone the much needed support.

The Downside of this Cancer, happened on his existing disease. It had gotten worse.

From being Independent in his daily routine, uncle became dependent on the family. His Huntington had gotten worse and the effects were quite visible. Manu then decided to take a 3 month sabbatical to be with his Dad and take care of him, while Panchhi put her heart and soul in his care and recovery.

She would prepare high protien food for him, but unluckily, his recovery wasn't happening as expected. But she never gave up. She kept feeding him healthy food and praying for his recovery. But as time went, uncle's condition became worse. He lost his voice and was almost bed-ridden.

This was around the time when Me and Manu met, and when I was back to Bangalore from Hyderbad, the first thing Manu wanted me to do was to meet his mom (Panchhi).

He knew having someone else to talk to would help her, but like any other girl, I was super scared to meet them so soon, but I dont know what convinced me and I went to meet Panchhi and uncle.

When I first saw her, she had such a sweet smile on her face! You could see that she is a calm, composed, gentle and loving person. And in no time, we connected.

I met uncle, and allthough he couldn't speak much, he remembered my name and called me by my name- Shrishti. You know, I still cherish that moment and that memory! And I always will.

Since then, I kept meeting Panchhi and it was always amazing. Once Uncle had developed some infection and had to be hospitalized for it. Upon asking Manu how can I help, he said, be with Mom that would be of great help, as she was alone in home. So after my office, I directly went to her and said, I am gonna stay with you untill uncle and Manu are back home. She was like, you have your office, you go, I am fine here.. and I said, I am staying with you even if you dont want me to....

And for the next 3 days, I stayed there. I just had work for friday and so when I got up to leave for work, she had prepared lunch tiffin for me. Moms!!!

I was speechless. It had been years since someone packed the tiffin for me and that too with home cooked food. I was like, so much is happening in her life, but the love she has is immense. It cannot go less. Its has become so rare to find such loving people. I felt lucky to have met her.

Time kept passing by, and I kept meeting them. Then we decided to call my parents here in Bangalore so that both the families can meet and we can go on a short trip somewhere.

So my parents came down to Bangalore, met Panchhi, uncle, Manu, Vicky and Panchhi's elder sister (Manu's masi). She is another amazing human and is a true rockstar

(that's what I call her). She came down from Dehradun so that Panchhi can go for the trip. You see, in all this, Panchhi had not been anywhere and so they insisted her to go on the trip.

But like I said, fate plays its card when you least expect it. We all had just reached Kerela when in the evening we got the news that Uncle passed away. Manu told me and then we told her together. We immediately flew back to Bangalore. All her relatives also flew to Bangalore for the last rites and rituals.

Trust me when I say it, I have never seen someone with so much love in her heart for everyone around her. My parents were in Bangalore for that week and even though she had gone through so much, she ensured that they felt comforted and loved.

So, one more instance here, depicting her care and love- On the 13th day after the last rites, food needs to be distributed in a temple to the priests. So pannchi and all of her relatives decided to cook food at home. The same day, one of my friend was travelling abroad forever and I had planned to see him off. Now, in all this, I knew my friend would understand and I did not feel like leaving their place. So I cancelled my plan. But upon hearing this, Panchhi said, "beta you go. Its important to meet your friend. We all are here". But I still just could not leave them and go. So anyways I did not go but the way she understood me and supported me, was something very big for me. My love and respect for her had grown immensely.

After all the rituals were done in Bangalore, Panchhi went to Dehardun for a month with her relatives, as all her maternal and paternal family is there. And plus it would give her some change. We knew Manu would have to change the home as it held too many memories for everyone.

She is a a strong lady. Her marriage, as I have mentioned was not an easy one. Be it the frequent moves, challenges of a new city or the fact that she could not work due to her responsibilities, she never ran away from anything and neither was afraid of anything. She knows how to live in the moment and make the most out of it.

The fact that her husband was diagnosed with a untreatable disease did not make her weak. Instead, she knew she had to be strong for the family. Moving to Bangalore, adapting to the city is not easy. People to come to the city for jobs have a hard time, but the determination she has, she knows how to make her way.

CHAPTER THREE

LIFE WITH US

While Pannchi was in Dehradun, I met Manu and he said, he would look for a new home now. His worry was that when he would go to work, Pannchi would be alone at home. All this while, she was occupied with uncle's care, food and stuff and so suddenly that change would be difficult for her

At that time, I was staying in a sharing flat with my other friends and I don't know what triggered this thought, but knowing her since all this while, I spoke to Manu and said what we we moved in together, like aunty he and I. We offcourse stay in different rooms, but that would give her more support and company.

I asked Manu to speak to her and meanwhile I spoke to my parents. My parents were ok with this decision and Panchhi also agreed. Yeah, moving in with future husband and Mother In law. So cool right! I knew Manu had spoken to her but I also thought of speaking to her once. I was once again amazed at her response. She said and I quote" Beta, why will I have any issues with this arrangement. I will have more family around me. I then asked her, what about your family, will they be okay with this ? To which she replied, there are only few people in my family who I respect and as long as they don't have any issues with this, I don't care about others". I was amazed at her thinking. She had so much clarity around what matters to her . That kind of clarity is what helps one decide to stay happy and peacefully.

While house hunting, we bonded even more. She would prepare food from home and get it for all of us. Panchhi even came to my home, where I was staying with my flatmates to help me pack. I did not have a lot of stuff but still, that mere thought made me feel special and loved. That's how Panchhi is. She makes people aroud her so comfortable.

So around September 2019, we all moved in together. Yes offcourse, It wasn't easy for her and for me also. Neither of us were used to this kind of arrangement. I had been staying away from my home since the past 9-10 years and she also wasn't used to this. So it was an usual, one of a kind set-up, which definitely proved fruitfull for all of us. Its because of that decision, we stand where we are- strong, united and together!

But yes, very honest, It was challenging initially. It was expected. We quarelled, cried together in lot of moments but there was always love!! I feel that is what is needed for every relationship.

She would say, when people stay together, frictions are bound to happen. But let's talk things out. She said, every day after dinner, let's all sit and discuss about our respective days, talk about any problem anyone has been facing so that, together we can help each other.

I came back to the phase of taking home cooked food in lunch boxes for office, evening tea ready made when we were back to home. She would try to interact with people around in the apartment, but would mostly be happy cooking for us. After long, I was getting home made food daily. I tell you, it was a luxury for me and still is!

We would decorate the house together. I would show her and order stuff online and what not.

Each day was different and fun for sure. As days passed, she would say, If only I could also be financially independent, did some job like you guys, it would help me be more productive. I knew she always wanted to work but never she had any opportunity, for n number of reasons. So we thought, this is the right time for her. She can also start something. We looked for options based on her interest and landed to one option- A home food delivery portal which onboards home chefs who prepare the food and then they get it delivered to customers.

We shared the idea with her and she loved it. We spoke to the team and they organized a food tasting with her, after which they would start with the Onboarding formalities. Panchhi was thrilled and axious, which is normal.

She took out her best cutlery, prepared the yummiest food and presented a super yummy lunch for the team. She was selected and we were elated. She landed her first job. What an amazing day that was!

I still remember, in the onboarding formalities, there was a medical fitness certificate needed and so when we went to the physician, she asked me, why do you need it? I said, my mother in law will be starting her job soon so it's a fomalility for that. She looked at Panchhi and said to her- Ma'am, you are an inspiration. I wish you good luck with your job. And the smile on her face was worth seeing. Starting her new job at 60! Super proud moment for everyone in her family. To mark that day, Manu and I got her an Aprot set, which she loved.

As soon as her onbarding completed, she started getting orders. For the initial one week, she needed some help with packing, managing the orders and stuff, but within a week, she was a pro. She learnt how to use the Ipad to check her orders and the menu. She was handling everything on her own. We would be away at work, and she would cook, pack and handover the food to the delivery guy.

She was happy and satisfied. When she recieved her first pay, you could see that spark in her eyes. Finally, after so long, she was doing what she had always wanted to do. Working and being financially independent.

And then, her journey as a home chef continued. We would recieved real time feedback and she would strive to improve with every meal. There were days when the Menu was new to her so she would read about the dish and then prepare it, with her twist and taste. She really was enjoying it.

Just then when it had been few months, covid hit us and we had to stop her home chef services due to the continous threat lingering around. We paused with the intention of starting again, but back then, who knew Covid would last that long.

Just when Covid had hit, I remember, even though I still was going to office, all of us were scared. Once Panchhi asked me- so you guys step out to have tea right! I said yes. And you know what she did- The next day when I was leaving for office, she gave me a thermos full of tea and said, now you all don't have to step out to have tea. You can have it in the office, don't risk going out. For a minute, I was speechless. I did not know how to react. That kind of care, thinking and efforts was just marvellous. I still have a smile on my face when I think about that Incident.

And then within next few days, all of us had started working from home and our life changed suddenly. I and Manu started working from home, which was again new for Panchhi but it gave the three of us more time together. We had stopped our house help as everything was so uncertain, so we would do all the chores together. But Panchhi would not let us get involved. She would be like, you have office work also, focus on that. I am there for all these things. And then finally we made a system- we divided work amongst the three of us so that it does not get too much for anyone.

Just when the 1st lockdown lifted, we started going out for early morning or late night walks in the society premises or nearby.

On one particular evening, she saw quite a few folks in the apartment getting food delivered. Since with covid, door step delivery was stopped, people had to step down to pick their food. She was like, if only they could also get homemade food with safety and hygiene and suddenly it hit us. What she was doing with another firm, she could do it herself, right here in the apartment, with more flexibility and control.

Manu and I discussed on the plan. We pitched in the Idea to her and she was on-board. She loved it! We spoke to the society assocation and they approved. That was it. Pannchi back in the food business, this time she had the menu in control.

We made a online poster telling about this venture to the apartment folks. We started with sunday evening snacks to see the response of the folks around and it was a huge success. We were not expecting that response. She prepared the food, we helped her pack and Manu and I delivered the food to people.

Everyone loved the food. We then started with both the weekends and included breakfast/lunch/dinner as well in the menu. People started recognizing Panchhi and we made new friends as well.

It was going well. Panchhi would brainstorm on the menu and we would help her with it. Our weekends during lockdown were the busiest but we all were loving it. It gave us immense sense of satisfaction and a feeling of achievement to Panchhi.

One anecdote here- There was this one guy in our apartment who loved Panchhi's home cooked food and would order everytime with us. We then got to know that he is leaving the apartment and would be moving someplace nearby. In the next few days, he calls us and says- Even though I have left the apartment, I would still want Panchhi's home cooked food. So whenever you guys are posting the menu just share with me as well and I will come pick it up. That is some fan following right! Panchhi was super happy.

And few of our friends also ordered food from her. Panchhi would prepare and they would either pick it up themselves or get it delivered. Such is the love people have for her food.

She even sent a friend of mine a home cooked meal thali on her birthday, along with a home made cake. I would have just mentioned how it was my friend's birthday and with this covid, we can't even meet her. And so , pannchi just made the food and said, send this to her. She will be happy! So we got the food delivererd to her and she was so happy. She called up and was crying. She said, no one has ever done this for me. I said, it was all panchhi and she was like, how cute aunty is. Well, that she is!

So things were looking really good and just when things started to pick up, there were a few covid cases detected in our apartment and for safety reasons, we had to pause our food delivery service.

Only when we thought of starting up again, My mom was diagnosed with Stage 4 Breast Cancer and things changed its course. I had to travel home for her treatment and the way Panchhi supported me was out of this world. I still remember when I was leaving for home, she said- "I know your being there with your mom is important right now, so you go and I will manage everything here" . Just listening to those words gave me the courage.

Now, during mom's initial chemotherapy, me and my sister decided to take turns for her treatment as we know it would be a long treatment. So while I was at home, taking care of things, I remember a surprise package arrived for me. And guess what it was- my favourite coconut ladoo and by now, I am sure you know who sent it. Indeed. Panchhi knew how much I love coconut ladoo and so she prepared them and sent it over! That might be a very small thing for her, but it meant the world to me.

Panchhi would regularly check on me when I was in Gurgaon.

Days passed and when my sister arrived after few months, I stayed with her for a week before travelling back to Bangalore. Now, before travelling to home for mom's treatment, she decided to have a court marriage done. You see things were very uncertain with respect to covid and with mom undergoing this long treatment, she knew this would give mom some relief. She suggested the same to me, that for now, have a court marriage. Now since Manu and I were staying together anyways, so it made sense to me.

When I was back to Banaglore, I discussed this with Manu and he was like, yes, instead of waiting endlessly, we should have a court wedding in Bangalore. We were skeptical discussing this with Panchhi but to our surprise, she was super supportive and totally onboard with the idea of us having a court marriage. She said, offcourse. Have the court marriage now and later when things setlle in terms of covid and my mom's treatment, we can have the rituals done. We were happy and I was amazed that my family and my new family both, are so open minded and cool!!

So we started with the formalities required for the same. Luckily I had friends in Bangalore who could be the witness during the wedding. Meanwhile, we decided to keep it small in our home, with us, Panchhi, Vicky and few of our common friends. Thats all! Even no one from my home could travel due to covid plus the situation at home, so I was feeling a bit low, that none of my family would be there, but Panchhi understood that. She took care of everything and ensured that I get the family support that I needed. I will tell you how.

To start with, when we went to shop for the wedding, I remember not being in the zone since things were tough back at home, but Pannchi being the awesome human she is, helped me with my entire shopping. Yes! She picked up dresses and suits and asked me to try them on. Not even once she said that go look for something. Infact, she would go around the mall and find some unique dresses for me to wear. I just had to try them on and then we finalized on it. Oh, I can't tell you how big of a relief it was. Everything that seemed difficult became easy because of Panchhi. And the best part, her choice matches my taste exactly. So now, whenever I need to shop, I take panchhi along and she gets me the best of clothes!

Also, for Mehndi, we had called a person home to put mehndi on my hands. I had Mehndi on both my hands and I remember Manu was out for some work. I got hungry and so, she fed me food. I still have that image in front of my eyes. She even put a little haldi on me and Manu, as a custom. Even though, it was just us, in our home, but it felt complete.

We decided to have Engagement at home, in the evening and court marriage the next day. During engagement, we had set up video calls with our families. It was lovely. For me the best part was, how supportive and understanding she was during our entire journey. She did not fuss over anything.

That is something I can never forget. She not just agreed, she ensured that both of us were happy. Such a blissful feeling it is.

When we got married, she was happy and so were we. We stayed together. But just within 10 days, I had to travel back home for Mom's treatment and yet again, Panchhi was there, being supportive as always. I had tears in my eyes, knowing I got another mother, who understands me and is there for me.

So, I travelled home and in a few days, when things were bit settled with respect to covid, Manu and Panchhi decided to go to Dehradun to visit her family since it was long they met. While they were there, Panchhi would regularly share pictures of everyone with me, made me talk to everyone over video calls. I felt included. Just then, while they were there, covid 2nd wave had peaked in the country. Unfortunately, Covid hit 4 out of 7 of her family members, including Manu and Pancchi.

I was scared. I was in home with mom and we all know the situation that it was everywhere in the country. I could do whatever I could from my home, but things were scary. Thankfully Panchhi had taken 1st dose of covid vaccine by then, so her symptoms did not worsen but I knew, mentally it would be tough for her. She would always say, more than covid impacting me physically, it will be difficult mentally to be quarantined for so long.

And so, staying in one room, all isolated was difficult for Panchhi. I remember how she would call me everyday and we would talk for hours. And she would call a lot of other folks as well, just so to not get the isolation to her head. She would keep herself busy by cleaning the room, talking to people. That's called resource and time management. No MBA will teach you that. There is one thing called acceptance and there is another thing called taking actions. Panchhi did both and by gods grace, everyone recovered and they were all healthy. I was relieved and then they decided to visit us in Gurgaon before heading back to Bangalore.

Initital few days when Manu and Panchhi came to our home, everything was good. Mom had her therapies continued and was recovering. But over the course, things became really tough on mom, mentally and we had to consult a new Psyciatrist. Mom has a history of depression and the treatment along with the medications was getting bit difficult for her. It was tough, to be honest.

Seeing mom's condition, Manu and Pancchi decided to extend their stay and that helped me big time to handle and take care of mom effectively.

Not just that, the way Panchhi would talk to my mom, explained things to her and take care of her, was something that I had not seen in my own family. Those two months were tough but I will always be grateful to Panchhi for being there. I was like, people don't do this much for their own family, this is in-laws we are talking about. You see, there was no ego, no drama, just pure love and affection.

Continuing about her anxiety that I spoke about in the earlier chapter, when we consulted Mom to a new Psychiatrist, Panchhi saw the difference in Mom and asked Manu for a consultation for herself. She said, I have been struggling with this problem for long now and if consulting the doctor can help, then why not. You know, this is when most people consider mental health issues a taboo, Panchhi openly talked about it and went to see the psychiatrist. She spoke to the doctor, told her about the issues lingering since long.

Not just that, her neice was also having trouble with anxiety, so Panchhi explained it to her and asked her to consult a Psychiatrist. I mean, I was amazed once again. Not only did she identified and acknowledged her problem, she took actions and trust me, she is doing much better now. That's the kind of thinking is missing in majority of folks, but she, like I said, knows what's important to her and puts her focus there.

Gradually with time, Mom got a little better and my sister was also planning to come down. So the three of us also planned our return and we came back to Bangalore together. It was good to be back to Bangalore, the three of us, after long.

I missed mentioning one point here. In all this, after our court marriage, Manu got an opportunity from his employer for an Onsite project in Canada. Manu asked me, and I said yes, go for it. I was still skeptical about my travel, given Mom's treatment and all, but I asked him to go ahead with the process. Even if I can't go, he should still go and explore this opportunity.

So when we were back to Bangalore, things were settling a bit back at home, mom was doing much better and we were little more confident about my travel and it was something we could explore, together.

This journey of staying with her, getting to know her was remarkable. The way she carries herself, the way she handled the covid situation, handled my mom, handled her anxiety, we all know it's not easy and not something we all see in our daily life. These are the things people run away from. They say, people get conditioned after a certain age, they are not open to new things. But Panchhi is not like that. On the contrary, she is more then willing and open to try new things, gain new experiences. The way she bonded with all of my friends is super amazing. Till date, whenever we speak or meet, they all would check on her and we would speak about her. Having that kind of love for people, doing things for them selflessly and not giving up, no matter what, is what makes Pannchi, the awesomest person, who is full of life.

CHAPTER FOUR

LIFE THEN

Now, came the next phase. If Manu and I were to travel to Canada, Mom would require to move to Chennai to stay with Vicky. We planned that move. Moved all our stuff to Chennai and Vicky also moved to a bigger place. Now, to give Mom that comfort and we all could stay together, I and Manu also moved to Chennai for few months. We wrapped things up in Banaglore and went ahead. Panchhi said, this moving frequently will not leave me. Just when she thought, Bangalore it is, there we were, moving again, to a new city, amidst new culture and people. Huh!

Leaving bangalore and moving to chennai was not an easy move. Vicky stayed in the outskirts of chennai and so availablity of things and having people around was not easy as it was in Bangalore. But it was the right thing to do. Anyways, we moved there.

Now, Chennai was a mixed emotion. On one side, Panchhi and Manu could stay with Vicky after long and I also had a chance to get to know him better. We were happy. We would explore nearby places and stuff. On the other side, the major issue that Pancchi faced was not having people around to talk to. We tried to go around and see if we could find some people , but it was difficult. It was a different setup. Majorly bachelors would stay there. Very few families and on top of it was the language barrier. So it was super difficult to find even few folks to rely. And probably that was our only worry when it came to panchhi staying in Chennai.

But, Panchhi being Pannchi, adjusted so well there as well. She would go on her own to the nearby market, and somehow not let the language barrier come in the way. I was once again amazed. Not just that, she even learnt how to make online payments for grocery and vegatable shopping as it was easy and convenient. When we, at a young age, feel slowed down or find it difficult to cope up, Panchhi always showed us the path and we felt, yes, its possible. And I think, thats why, having no known person around, still we were able to stay there.

Manu and I celebrated our first Karwachauth in Chennai and I felt more than us, Panchhi was excited. You know, ever since we started staying together, Panchhi never ever asked or expected me to do pooja, fast or get involved in any religious stuff that she is into. No, I am not an atheist. I do believe there is a higher power governing the universe but anyways, so yeah. She is very understanding that way. But karwachauth is one festival she wanted me to celebrate properly and that's the least I could do for her. Also, it's a day to celebrate love for your husband so why not. And Manu also fasted with me, so in all fairness, I enjoyed it.

She took me shopping and bought me a new lehenga and matching kurta pajama for Manu.

I remember endlessly waiting for the moon to come up, but it was raining heavily. She only said, just wait for half n hour more and then see moon over a video call and complete your fast. Well, that's what I am talking about. She is super understanding and practical at the same time. She then prepared food for us to have post the fast.

Then came Diwali. I remember during Diwali, finding the basic pooja items or prasad was difficult there. So, she would be like, it's fine. She would come up with some or the other alternative to use. That's what the mindset should be. She would not get stuck on what is not available, instead she would look for ways around to make it work.

In Chennai as well, her day would start early. She would prepare breakfast and lunch tiffin for vicky and, when we would not eat breakfast properly, saying he is getting late. she would get upset. She then remembered how for my mom, we would prepare smoothies which would provide a whole balanced nutrition in one meal and so, she asked me to teach her the same. I told her the ingredients. And there it was. A glass of smoothie, ready for vicky for his breakfast. He could not say no to that as it was just one glass. She was then bit relieved. Not only that, she also enjoyed drinking smoothies herself. She would experiment, combine different base, fruits and sweetner to see what works and would try that.

Rest, during the day, she would do household chores, watch TV/mobile, and get occupied preparing food for everyone. She never complained about the hot and humid temperature, language barrier or a lot of other stuff, about which we would daily complaint and crib about. She would often say, if you have to do this, might as well do it with a smile, it will make it less difficult. So true right. We also had to stay there, might as well do it right.

Also, she loves beaches. And being in chennai, we tried to go around beaches over the weekend, which would be a good change for her and for everyone.

Time went by, and so gradually, I became all the more sure about my travel as well, but since I was to serve my notice period in my current organization, we decided that Manu would travel first, and I would join him in a month or two. Pannchi had some dental treatment pending so we decided that I will get that started and then travel to Canada.

Things were really looking up. This move to Canada was something that would not only help Manu and me, but down the line, Vicky also planned to move there and Panchhi would also come along. She got super happy with the idea of moving to Canada. I guess, for her, it was more like, if my kids are happy, I will be happy.

When Manu was supposed to fly, I and Pannchi flew to Delhi to see him off. Vicky had to attend a friend's brother wedding so he could not join us. Now since we were going to Delhi, Panchhi and I decided to stay back for a few days since my parents stay in Gurgaon and her elder sister and family also stayed there. So we were like, lets stay here for few days and then we will fly back to Chennai.

I kept meeting her there and we all, like my family and her family even got together once for one big family get together. Her family shares the same warmth, same love. It was a good get together and we all really enjoyed each others company.

Just when we were supposed to head back, a day before, Pancchi called up in the evening and was crying. I was confused. I was like what happened, why are you crying ? She was like, Vicky is in the hospital and there is no one there with him. I told her, we will fly right away to Chennai and be with Vicky, don't worry. Just then when I was about to leave to meet Panchhi, we got the most horrible news of our lives. Manu's cousin called me and said that Vicky is no more. Those words shook me from inside. I just fell on the floor and had no clue what happened. I was in my parents home, Pannchi was at her sister's place and Manu was in Canada.

When we left him in Chennai, he was all well. We even spoke a few days back. I was shattered. I could not muster any courage to call up Manu or face Panchhi. In no time, everyone in Panchhi's family got the news. Manu had also known before I could tell him and when he called , I told him, just come back!

I immediately went to Pannchi and I was horrified. Manu's cousins had not told her yet. She was told that he is not well and is in a Hospital. They said, we would not be able to console her. Let Manu come back, only then we will tell her.

Now, since Vicky passed away in his office, and there was no legal guardian there, they wanted any one family member to come over for the formailities, before we could bring him to Gurgaon. With Manu travelling back and Panchhi not aware of anything, me and Manu's friend went to Chennai for the formailties. Panchhi would call to check that where was I, why weren't we going to Chennai and all those numerous questions. I could not even talk to her. I knew she would catch my lie in no time.

I asked Manu's cousin to be there with her all the time.

Meanwhile, we flew to chennai . It took us one full day there to complete the process and by that time, Manu had also reached home in Gurgaon. Panchhi's other relatives had also come down to Gurgaon. When we were about to reach back, Manu told Pannchi. She was in pain. She was angry, upset. There were numerous questions in her mind. That's bound to happen. All of us had so many questions bothering us.

I did not really want to talk about it, given how painful it is. But during Vicky's funeral, I was with Panchhi the whole time and she said this one line- Ja beta Ja, teri maa khush reh legi! " Go son go, your mom will be happy here"

I looked at her in disbelief. How do people gather so much strength! I had this feeling of immense respect for her. She is an epitome of strength, life and love.

Days after that were a blur. We then went to Dehradun for the final rituals and due to covid, extended our stay there for 2-3 months.

She would cry, try to hide her pain but it's inevitable. You know what helped. A Dog. Yes! Manu's family in Dehradun have a pet dog (called Oreo) and he became our source of happiness for the time we were there. Panchhi would take him out for walks, feed him and we would play with him. All of us would involved with him and spend our time with him.

Once we even took Oreo for a picnic and was super happy and so were we. I still can't imagine what would we have done if Oreo wasn't there. Since we were there in winters, she said, lets buy him some nice jacket so went and shopped for Oreo. We even took oreo for a spa once. He did not like it, but we enjoyed spending that time with him.

And see her love. Even after going through all this, Panchhi told us, you guys continue your plan to Canada, I'll stay in Dehradun and run a PG from my home, afterall I could never stay there and this is a chance to stay there. But at that moment, Manu and I decided to stay back in India with Panchhi, because taking her along, so far, was not an option and neither leaving her behind was an option.

Many of our friends and family questioned this move, but we were sure of it. I continued in my current organization and Manu took the tranfer back to India office. Being with family was important for everyone.

I was amazed to see how amazing and helpful Manu's family is. For those next few months, everyone was there. It felt so blessed. I believe that's the support one needs in their life to overcome any difficulties in life. That support and love is unconditional.

CHAPTER FIVE

LIFE NOW

When the question of our next move came to our mind, we were confused whether to stay back in Dehradun or be back to Bangalore. But after a lot of thinking, we decided to come back to Bangalore.

So, when Covid settled a bit, we came back to Bangalore, afterall it's this place that we all can relate to. Being in Bangalore was a good change for all of us. We stayed in a BnB, since we first had to find a house on rent in Bangalore and then get our stuff from Chennai. The stay was a welcoming change. We would cook food, meet our known people and spend majority of our time in house hunting. Our first preference when it came to looking for a home was it should be in a society so that all of us can find people to talk to and interact, but mostly for Panchhi we knew that enviornment was important.

Here I have another example of strength for you- During all those house hunts and people who stay in Bangalore know how painful it is, she went along with us to each one of them. Also, the BnB we were staying in was little far, so it was quite a travel each day. But she never backed down.

And we preferred that. She would give her inputs, at times make jokes about the high rents and we tried to make a day out of those house hunts. That is some life spirit she has which makes her so different and special at the same time.

Luckily, through one of our close friends, we finally found a place. A short story here- When we had just entered to meet the owners and see the flat, at first seeing me and Manu, the owner was little skeptical but the moment she saw Pannchi, she was like, mother haan. Now my home would be maintained!! We still laugh at that. I think its the aura, the vibe panchhi has. Her smile, her lovely face, it just makes people so comfortable.

Panchhi loved the Kitchen (her happy place), we loved the balconies. In short,after so many months of staying here and there, not having that personal space, we finally found a place we all could call Home. It was a good feeling.

Now, that we finalized the house, we knew the next difficult part was in line. Actually two difficult part. First one was that we had to go to Dehadun for Manu's cousin's wedding (Panchhi's brother's son). Manu and I were not very sure if going there would be a good idea or how will it be on Panchhi emotionally, but she wanted to go, afterall she loves her brother and how could she miss his nephew's wedding.

So we travelled back to Dehradun and Panchhi took part in all the celebrations. At the wedding, it was super difficult for me, for manu and I could not even imagine how difficult it would have been on her. But not even once, she showed that. It was like, she forgot her own pain for her family's happiness. I don't know how she does that, but during such tragedy, when people become bitter, she became filled with more love and happiness.

After the wedding, we flew back to Bangalore and stayed in another BnB for a week or 2, untill we had the house ready. Now, was the time for the second difficult part. Going to Chennai to get our stuff back to Bangalore.

Manu and I, had once already travelled there for some legal formalities, but for Pannchi it would be the first time. It was the house that we created so many memories in, even though it was for few months.

Anyways, Pannchi and we went there. The moment she entered the home, she cried and cried, saw Vicky's stuff and cried again. It was important. That closure probably was needed. All of us cried there. And somehow we gathered courage and started with the packing. Movers and packers were there and in a day or two, we were done with the packing and all. Leaving that home was difficult but in order to move ahead, one needs to leave things back.

We came down to Banaglore and our stuff also reached here. It felt as if we have been packing and moving for quite some time now. I just could not stop thinking on how Panchhi has been moving around every 3-4 years. I realised it's not at all easy. Anyways, after all these months, settling down again looked humungous but we took it slow. With time, all of us felt little sorted and bit stable.

Good part about this home- We had quite a few known friends close by, so having them around helped big time.

It was still bit difficult initially for Pannchi, because it was the routine again. It needed efforts for her to get out of the bed, but she was doing it. On top of it, her dental treatment, that had been pending since long, finally started . So the fact that all of her teeths were removed, stepping out became a difficulty for her. She was too conscious and that was natural. We understood but somepart of us wanted her to meet people. Apart from that eating and all was also difficult.

But as they say, life will always give you happy moments. And there we had, the happy moment we all were waiting for. The apartment we moved in, celebrated all the festivals and to our joy, we found that on one of the days in the celebration, residents were invited to set up food stalls in the apartment. The moment I saw it, I knew it. I told Pannchi and she was elated. Scared but elated.

We enquired about the same and gave Panchhi's name. She even came up with super amazing food items to present at the stall. I believe, that is why having that one thing (be it a hobby or a regular work) that gives you joy and happiness is so important. She did not think twice before saying yes to this. And that became a major distraction for her.

She began the preparations and on the day of the event, all of us were there with Panchhi to help her. To our surprise, the response to her food stall was amazinggg!! People loved her foood. People loved that how everything was made from scratch and out of love. And you know the best part, people started recongnizing her. While waiting for the food, they would talk to her and she was talking happily to them. Her initial inhibition of talking with no teeth was shattered and there she was , smiling and cooking! Ohh, I can't tell how, how happy and heartfull we were feeling.

I believe, it's since then, she doesn't shy away from stepping down for a walk or going out to eat, or meeting people in general.

Ohh and yes, Pannchi and I even took part in Antakshri competition held in the apartment. Getting up on the stage is scary for everyone and she, for the very first time in her life, was up on the stage and she enjoyed every bit of it. She even said, we will take part in this everytime. I was thrilled and amazed. Her take on life is phenomenal and I feel that, a lot of my growth and positivity, comes from her. And in all sense I am truly blessed.

And then in a month or so, one more of food stall event happened and happily she took part in it. It was a competition this time, and she came 4th out of 10. We celebrated her that day. After coming back, she even had ideas for the next time a food stall event happens. Super cute she is!!

In the next few months, we took few trips, all 3 of us. It helped. It helped us bond better. Let me tell you one more story about a very random trip to Goa. One of Manu's friend asked to join him for a trip to Goa for 4-5 days and I and Pannchi said, yes, Go!! He hadn't met him in long, so it would be a good change for him also and what place better than Goa. He had his tickets booked and all, and one fine day he said, I am anyways going there, why don't you both join me when I am done with my part of trip. It striked us, yes why not. It would be a good family holiday and since Pannchi had always wanted to visit Goa, it was a good idea.

Well, the plan was on. We made all the bookings. Now, Manu travelled on thursday and we were supposed to travel on Monday. The weekend between was one amazing weekend I had. Literally! Panchhi and I lived like Bachelors for those 2 days. True!! We found one amazing webseries to Binge watch on and we spent the weekend watching the series, discussing it (oh, thats so important), eating (sometimes we would cook or we would order). It was amazing!! I felt as if I am staying with my flatmates. Panchhi, the coolest Mother In Law. I was amazed on how fast the weekend went.

And coming to Goa. She once again proved how cool and understanding she is. Our Goa trip was in between Karwachauth and that is something we all look forward you. Even though Manu and I fast, we still enjoy the feel and warmth of the festival. Initially Panchhi said, It's Karwachauth, you two should be in Bangalore to celebrate it properly, but we convinced her. It would be so cool to celebrate it in Goa, afterall what matters is that we are together. She understood and bought me a nice ethnic dress to wear for the day. I shopped for the other things required for that day.

I packed my ethnic wear and a whole lot of other Indian stuff to Goa. On the day of karwachauth, she was so excited. With whatever we could find in Goa, we celebrated the festival. We went to the beach all dressed up in Indian wear and she became our photographer. She clicked some amazing pictures of us on the beach. And not only that, she would tell us different poses, afterall we are very bad at that. She would teach us and enjoy that! Oh, such an amazing day that was.

She even bought few trendy clothes in Goa and wore them to beaches. Few days we would cook in the BnB we were staying in and few days we would eat outside. She was so adapting there in Goa. When I and Manu would take a walk on the beach, she would sit on those beach chairs and just relax. Not once she said no to any experience there in Goa.

And that is the best part. She is very open to experiences and ideas. She isn't stuck in the old age thinking and traditions. She keeps an open mind and has adapated well to the current times. I believe that is the reason we three share this bond.

And there is Grit and Determination. Let me tell you about that as well- On our next trip to Amritsar and Kartarpur, on the third day, Panchhi fell sick. She caught viral, a bad one. We took rest that one day, she ate home cooked food and did all the natural remedies that were needed. For a moment, we thought we might have to cut the trip short, as after long, she fell this sick. But there was one motivation in her head- I have to go visit the Golden temple. I have come so far and won't go back without visiting it. And trust me when I say that, It was like Magic. The next day, she felt so better that we not only went to Golden temple, but walked around for shopping, eating food and what not and she was all fine.

You know, till date, in the past and now as well, many of our friends had come over to meet us and not even once Panchhi said, let's order food or you guys cook. The moment we mention that some friends are coming over, her mind goes- ok so what do I cook? Even when we say we will order, she is like- NO!! They are coming home, I will make something. That thing which requires so much efforts and time, seem so easy to her. Even on Manu's birthday, I had called a lot of friends over. So I insisted that we order, afterall cooking for so many people is difficult. But I am sure you all know by now how Panchhi is.. She cooked for all of them. I could only negotiate that will order roti and 1 curry from outside, rest everything she prepared. And no, she was not tired at all. Infact, she was super happy. She set the entire table, took out her best cutlery and everyone enjoyed ! She added that homely touch!

She is currently completing her dental treatment. Its tough. Those frequent visits to the dentist, trying on multiple dentures, getting used to the denture and so on! The next steps in the treatment is to have a surgery and implanting those dentures permanently. It's a long treatment and there are days when Panchhi has her doubts, but the good thing is that she is vocal. She would speak to us about her apprehensions and we would ask the doctor to speak to her. You know, it is so important to let your thoughts out, and to not let them become negative. Best part is that she understands that! She would often joke around, when will I get my teeth and I will eat Golgappa! It's been so long I had one and we all would laugh. We tell her, there- you have your motivation. Complete the treatment and eat as many golgappas as you want!

Eating without teeth is not easy and she has been doing it for the last 6 months! Hats off to her. And in those last 6 months, we took several trips, outings, restaurant vists but not once she said no to any of it. She has found her way to eat food and so has been able to enjoy those trips and outings. That's one major learning for all of us- Don't wait for life to be perfect, enjoy it at every moment. Just like how she is doing- eating the icecream before it melts.

She also is making efforts to go for walks daily. Recently she made some friends in the apartment and is enjoying their company. She now puts efforts to go outside daily, walk a bit and then meet them. She would come back and tell us all about her evening with them. I was the happiest when she told how she met people and made friends with them. The reason we moved in to a bit far off apartment was the fact that she could meet new people and when she did, it felt real good. She says, teach me how to save contact numbers on my phone and I will ask them for their numbers. Also, she is in all plans of pitching in the idea of having get-togethers to them. Wow!! I jokingly tell Manu, we did not make such group yet here and look at her, she found her tribe! But we are happy. That "me" time is important for everyone and I am glad she also realises that.

Since I have resumed office, she gets up early in the morning to prepare breakfast and lunch for me. I told you know, it's all about love. When I come back from work, we talk, a lot. She tells me about her day, complaints about Manu (and I love that by the way) and asks me about my day. When I had gone for the very first day, I asked her- How was your day? What did you do? And she said- I was bored, you weren't there ! I love her.

Now, the next plan, in our minds, post her treatment is getting her into the home food business. She loves cooking, has done this before, so why not. Also people in the apartment already recognize her and her cooking so that's an advantage.

But here, look at her thinking. It' so entrepreneurial. So, there is a new corporate office coming up near to our apartment. She keeps saying, buy me a food cart, I will also go sell tea and snacks there. You both go to office and I will spend my day there. Just the thought inspires us. At this age, when women think that they will just relax now, she knows the importance of working and keeping herself occupied. She herself says, let me work untill I can. Afterall, that's how I will remain fit, physically and mentally. The food cart idea shows how much inclined and interested she is to do something on her own. That is a possibility we will explore. Afterall, we know, she can handle things very well on her own.

She now wants me and Manu to have a proper wedding with the pheras. For someone who was so cool and supportive with our live in arrangement and the court wedding, having the proper Intimate traditional wedding is something that is important. We all want that. We plan to have it later this year.

You know, It's because of her, Manu and I are able to eat healthy, focus on our health. If you leave it to us, we will end of ordering from outside most of the time. Even if the work is too much, we know home cooked meal is a possibility. So you remember, as kids, our moms would cut fruits and give it to us, on the table. It is like that now as well for us. There are days when we eat fruits ourself and on some days when we forget, she never forgets to bring those fruits to us. I feel loved and blessed at those moments. Good thing is, now, unlike earlier, she eats it herself too. She understands the importance of eating healthy and so now makes efforts on that side. Often, she will quit sugar in tea and replace with Jaggery, some days she will eat Oats for breakfast and on some days, she will eat dates for sweets instead of actual sweets. She tells us, how in her post graduation in home-science, they were taught about carbs, protiens, fats and all that. And so, when we talk now, she often talks about importance of eating greens, fruits etc. She also, very often, tries new recipes. Some after watching in Youtube and some, using her own imagination and creativity.

We even tried something new on social media. We asked her to record small video/reels with tips and trips from her Kitchen experience. We started off and she did so well. Public speaking, that too on a video is scary for majority of us. She too was scared. But she practiced, and she rocked it. She would practice what she needs to say and then record the video. She kept a diary of all such ideas and said, she would make videos on these ideas. Commendable!

And you know what- she is the one who motivated me to learn riding scooty and driving a car. She often says, even if you don't ride it daily, you should learn these skills. It makes you more independent and comes in handy throughout your life. She says- I could never learn it but it's something I wanted to learn. And when I bought a scooty, she was the happiest. She sat with me, even when I was not very confident and I took her around the apartment. She showed so much confidence in me.

Point is, like I said earlier, she is very open to new ideas. She watches Shark Tank and says, we can also do this. Let's start something and then we will also go there. She is someone who embraces technology, unlike many others. Apart from social media, she learnt NetBanking, making online payments and transactions, online shopping etc. She would keep checking clothes/kitchen appliances and ask us, shall I order this for you guys? Super sweeet!

And Financially also she is sound. She keeps a track of her pension, her expenditures, her investments. She would check the app now and then and ask Manu all the questions she has. I am really impressed with this. She for one, not only keeps track but would like to know about any activity happening in her account. She taught us the importance of saving money, reducing wastage and buying only when necessary. I know there is a mindset difference, but I believe we tend to forget these things and having those elders around to remind us is really needed.

You know, things are like totally opposite here at our crazy home. So, in today's changing times, kids don't prefer staying with parents while parents want to stay with kids. In our case, it's the opposite. We just cannot imagine living without her and she would often say- you both stay here, I will go to Dehradun and start a PG there! We will agrue with her everytime she says this. We tell her, we love staying with you. It makes our life so easy, happy and loving. There is no other way we would have it. Afterall, you won't find such lovely flatmates anywhere!!

For Christmas last year, she decided to send gifts for all the small kids in the home. She said, it will be a suprise. We helped her pick the gifts and she ordered them. Upon recieving the gifts, everyone was so happy. For a while they all were confused as to who sent it and she was enjoying all that. She said we won't tell them, let them guess!! But eventually they got to know that their Panchhi Nani had sent those gifts. So thoughtful.

Oh and yes, by the way, last year for new year celebration, we did it in Pannchi's style. We all decided to go old school and the way she loves it. So, we all picked up a meal we would cook ourselves. No ordering in, no going out, just good home cooked meal. You would have remembered from her childhood chapter about how they used to celebrate new year. So Manu cooked a starter, she prepared the main course and I went for the dessert. We had the food ready by 8-8:30 PM. We then put up a movie online, laid out mattress and there we all were, all cozied up, watching the movie and eating. She enjoyed that! She told everyone how it was like good old days, except that she couldn't eat peanuts and chikkis now (joking about her dental treatment) but yes, it felt good. We even danced after the movie and she, as I say, is a sport. She danced so well! I am gonna make sure she dances to a full song in our wedding. I know she will !

Now, apart from all things good, there are issues as well. There is generation gap, mindset difference and different thought process and I know it's natural. It's bound to happen. I won't sugarcoat it. But you know the good part. She always strives to clear the air. You know how stuffy and difficult it gets when that cold war happens in any home. And none of us really want that. So even in case of any misunderstanding, she is very open to listening. We would talk and sort stuff out. Even just now, on new year eve, she said. I have taken a resolution- I will not jump to any conclusion when someone says anything. I will try to understand their perspective, if needed, talk to them and clarify stuff. I won't assume and spoil my mood. This is something, many of us fail at. And she, realises this and makes efforts to avoid that. Ins't it commendable.

You see, clashes are obvious when any two people stay together. But as long as everyone is open to talk to, it works out. Clashes can also become fun. It's all about thc attitude. And I am thankfull Panchhi also shares the same attitude.

I for one, share a very special bond with her. We live in a society wherein since forever, we have always heard this notion that a Mother In Law and a Daughter In Law cannot go along, cannot have a happy and loving relationship. We break this norm. I myself was told by many that after your marriage, things will change. Panchhi will change. That's how it happens. Mother in law's change. But you know what? Nothing changed. Our bond has only gotten better and stronger. I have literally found another Mother in Pannchi. And the way she takes care of me is phenomenol. We often say, we are friends. I can talk to her about anything and everything under the sky. Be it about marriage, general news, periods, kids and what not. I know, there is no filter now between us.

We go for spas, massages and shopping together and it's so much fun. I used to do it with my Mom and now I ensure that Panchhi also pampers herself. We make her try and buy funky clothes and she will give it a try for sure. She says- I now have to buy a Jeans and wear once! And we will do that soon...

And not once will she ask me to contribute in any household chores when I am working, be it work from home or from Office. Manu and I, at times, will force her that we will share the workload and then she is like- you both are working, you have office work, let me handle this. She is very clear on this- be it the guy or the girl, if one is working, household work gets difficult for them to handle. She will always say, girls after marriage often quit their jobs but you know, they shouldn't. If needed, they should take leave without pay and see how can things be managed but should never leave their job. That is what gives them financial independence to face life and earn the respect.

She will often tell about her many relatives who did the same mistake. I really admire this outlook she has. If all the daugher in laws get such understanding mother in laws, it gets so easy to handle work, their own home and this home. All that support that we need is right there.

Staying with her, listening to her stories, I have realised that accepting whatever comes to your life is so important and so is moving on. Unless you accept your current situation, you won't be able to move past that. And you won't be able to work for the future. She is someone who has never shied away from any of her responsibilities, no matter how hard it was. She always gave it her 100%. And at the same time, she never lost her passion and dedication when it comes to following her dreams. She still has it inside her. When she talks about it, the way her eyes beam with Joy and happiness, tells everything. That kind of passion I may not have, But I want to help her achive and fulfill her passion. Afterall, it is never too late to achieve your dreams.

She keeps our home lively, in true sense.

Live, Love, Laugh

These words- Live, Love, Laugh: are the essence of our life. This is what gives our life meaning and motive. You know everytimc I look at Pannchi, and think about the different phases of her life, I see love, strength, resilience and dedication. Her life has been full of struggles and challenges and still, you see that child like excitement in her when she talks about her interest and passion.

"

Her Childhood teaches us commitment, sense of responsibility, clarity of thoughts and acceptance. No comparison, just being happy in what you have and yet striving for excellence.

Her life after her marriage teaches us love, maturity, never giving up and dedication. Accepting all that comes your way, making it fun and loving and finding a way to cherish and relive those memories.

Her life with us teaches us open mindedness, compassion, passion, support and always looking up in life. Following your passion, no matter at what age, learning technology and not shying away from it.

Her life now teaches us acceptance, strength and love. Actually a lot more. Expressing your emotions, taking help when needed and being there for your family."

We all agree.. Life is hard for everyone. Our challenges might differ but it's all in the individual attitude that makes the difference. It is that attitude which defines how he/she takes on those challenges. In every difficult situation we face we always have two ways- either to give up or to rise up. Panchhi also had many such difficulties in her life but she always chose the path to rise up. She always kept her calm and went ahead with whatever life threw at her.

Even now, she does the same with equal calmness and perseverance. She keeps her roots intact and still progresses with the world. She teaches us a lot through her life experience and at the same time is very open to learning from any and everyone. She knows when to bend the rules and when to follow them.

I don't know about the future, but as of now, Panchhi is trying to capture every moment of her life, with her loved ones. She often says no one knows about the future, life is so uncertain, so don't wait for the future to enjoy things. Yes, there are days, when she is low, but she keeps herself occupied with some or the other work.

If I recollect her life journey, at every phase, she has faced numerous challenges, difficulties and struggles. And still, if you meet her, you will see a genuine smile on her face, genuine care and love in her heart and genuine concern in her mind. That is how she is. Still the same! Always up for life, no matter what! Our generation gets bothered by the silliest thing and look at them, so gracefully dealing with major setbacks of life. She has overcome and achieved so much and when you acknowledge it, they are like- what's there in this?

"This attitude is what makes life more fun".

And as I pen down my last thoughts, I would like to tell you all that I am beyond grateful to have met Panchhi. No matter what has happened in the past, our life now is filled with love, laughter and happiness. A lot of credit for it would go to Panchhi. She supports us. She gets along with all of our friends. She understands us. Whenever we speak of trying something new, she understands our motive behind, gives her ideas and always motivates us. I am more than glad that now, after all this, she has understood the importance of self-care. So, she makes sure to find time for herself.

You know, life will give you shocks and surprises. We cannot even plan the next ten minutes of our life. So seize every moment. And once you are done reading this book, I hope you found some hope and inspiration. And now, take a moment, and look around and find such inspirations in your life. I am sure you will find many. That's the beauty and simplicity of it. You don't really need to look outside for inspiration, most of the times it's there around us. I feel they need more recognition. Afterall, real education is not taught in schools/colleges, it's in their life. Their life journey!

Lines from "Life Is", by Mother Teresa-

"*Life is an opportunity, benefit from it.*"

"*Life is beauty, admire it.*"

"*Life is a dream, realize it.*"

"*Life is a challenge, meet it.*"

Untill, we meet again, let Panchhi's life give you the inspiration you were looking for. Let it create hope and help you overcome whatever is stopping or slowing you down. You can pause for a day, but don't ever stop, never stop learning, afterall life will never stop teaching . Be a good student and you will do wonders. Love more passionately, smile more heartily and laugh out loudly.

To Pannchi- I Love You. I may not say it often, but I love you. In you I have found a friend, a mentor, a mother and so much more. I am beyond grateful to the universe for you and this book is a tribute to you, for all you have done and for all that you do. Keep rising and growing like you have always done and keep being the awesome self that you are. You might not know it yourself but you are a super woman who inspires many around her. Much more power, strength and love to you.

9 798889 593126

Printed by Libri Plureos GmbH in Hamburg, Germany